Contents

Quilting Counts! 2

Hand or Machine Stitch? 5

Elegant & Powerful Straight Lines 7
    Not All Lines Are Equally Visible   9

Decoding the Magic of Lines 10
    Visibility   10
    Style   11
    Scale   12

Getting Started 13
    Line Choices   16
    Outline Quilting   16
    Vertical and Horizontal Lines   19
    Diagonal Lines   20
    Plaid or Broken Plaid Lines   20
    Staggered Lines   21
    Random Lines   21

Marking Lines 22
    Painters Tape   22
    Quilting Paper   24
    White Chalk Wheel   26
    No Marking   26

In Conclusion 28

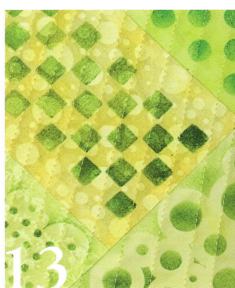

Quilting Counts!

Quilting through the layers is essential to the overall success of any quilt and yet, oddly, is often overlooked. How many times have you meticulously followed a quilt pattern only to discover the last step is "quilt as desired"? How unhelpful! The right choice of quilting design can move any quilt one big step toward stardom or an equally big step in the opposite direction. No one wants to go to the effort of putting time and money into a quilt and then be disappointed in the result. This book will help you decide how to maximize the 'wow' factor of your quilt by using the right stitching in the right way and in the right places.

Really, when you think about it, it's the stitching through the layers that transforms a top into a quilt, so make sure it contributes in full measure to the beauty to your quilt!

One general rule of thumb to keep in mind is that the amount of quilting needs to be adequate in order to hold the layers together. This choice is driven by both the quilt's ultimate function

Calm colors and simple piecing make this top a perfect partner for some dynamic straight line quilting. The light colored fabrics will show the quilting off to great advantage.

Design A. *This quilting design would be easy to sew but that's about the only good thing to say for it. It's boring and doesn't enhance the quilt top.*

Design B. *Suddenly things are looking up. A more interesting idea makes this top start to really come to life. It will very likely need more stitch lines, in order for the quilt to remain square and straight.*

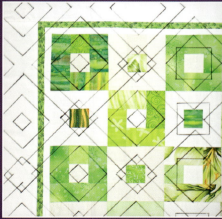

Design C. *Taking the ideas from the design above and adding to it has done the trick. The quilting compliments the top and certainly gives it a stronger visual appeal than it could ever have without it.*

Penthouse View. *Quilted using design C but with a few added boxes to even out the quilting makes this exactly right. 'Boxes within boxes' is a more complex design than we started experimenting with and adds interest without overwhelming the piecing. The quilt design was marked with masking tape then stitched with a thin, variegated polyester thread.*

and the batting used. A quilt that is meant to be used on a bed will need to have more quilting in order to hold up well to a lot of use and multiple washings. A quilt intended to be displayed isn't likely to need as much quilt stitching, unless, of course, the overall artistic design requires it.

Batting manufacturers offer advice on how densely to quilt which is sometimes helpful but can also lead you straight into trouble. The batting package may advise that the quilting can be up to 10" apart but will that small amount of thread support the weight of the water when washing a large quilt? Probably not. Some 100% cotton batts require that you quilt lines between one-half and one inch apart in order to avoid fiber migration or bunching. Other types of batting can be quilted more sparingly. So by all means look at the manufacturer's recommendations and then make your own determination of how much quilting is optimal.

Another good idea is to make sure the density of the quilting is uniform across the surface. Quilts not stitched evenly often ripple, sag and won't hang flat. They wave at the bottom.

If the border isn't quilted about the same amount as the center it tends to look like the quilter ran out of time which is probably not the intended message.

Modern quilters are often quite nostalgic about antique hand-stitched quilts but may not be able to say exactly what it is that appeals to them. I suspect that part of the reason we love them so much is that the old style of batting necessitated heavy, all-over stitching in order to avoid fiber migration, which is unattractive and makes the quilt less warm. So our foremothers stitched and stitched until there was simply no room for pills or bunching to form in their batting. The result? Really lovely quilts!

Tip!

If areas on your quilt puff up unattractively, just quilt more lines across those places. Many times adding a diagonal line through a section will solve the problem. You can also repeat a design that is already stitched into the quilt, such as adding a square within a square.

Hand or Machine Stitch?

Both machine and hand stitched quilting have wonderful qualities and multitudes of admirers. Many quilters choose one method or the other based upon their skill, inclination or the design requirements of their quilt, all of which are perfectly reasonable factors to consider in making this important decision. Mixing the two techniques is also very effective with the right design.

If you enjoy hand stitching and have the time to commit to it, you can create beautiful quilts. Since only one thread is used, the quilted lines are a subtle series of dots or dashes that very delicately make their way over the quilt surfaces. The texture created is very pleasing to the eye. Hand stitching is much friendlier to a design with multiple starts and stops, which can quickly become tedious to a machine stitcher. And its easy portability makes it the obvious choice for the quilter who wants to travel – be it from one country to another or just from room to room.

Machine quilting is very popular. Part of the reason has to do with the much shorter time it takes to finish a project relative to the time it would take to hand quilt. Modern sewing machines tempt quilters with a variety of helpful features such as stitch length regulation, feed dogs that disengage at the touch of a finger and walking feet that make it easy to feed a bulky quilt under the needle. Not to mention an enticing variety of programmable stitches. Another advantage, I believe, is that machine stitching tends to be a bit more durable because two threads are in play, not just one. Because it is a continuous line of thread on both the top and bottom of the quilt, it generally makes a much bolder design statement.

When deciding between machine and hand stitching, take a moment to look at your quilt top. Which technique better lends itself to the authenticity of the quilt? Which do you prefer to sew? Will either hand or machine stitching be significantly simpler for the particular quilting design you have settled upon? For example, a series of small, concentric squares would be much more easily stitched by hand. When you finished one square it would be simplicity itself to slip the needle between the layers and come up again where the next square is to start. Machine stitching small squares could be tiresome as each one would start and stop independent of the next.

Neither technique is more desirable than the other. They each offer different design possibilities. When well planned and carefully stitched, quilting by either method results in a beautiful, expressive quilt.

Elegant & Powerful Straight Lines

Fully integrated and thoughtfully planned quilting enhances and supports the quilt. By integrated, I mean that the quilted stitch design should tell the same story as the quilt's composition.

This top is an example of squares, squares and more squares. When considering how to quilt a top, one trick that often works is to think of the overall idea the quilt conveys. Here it could be pink flowers surrounded by grass. With that thought in mind, let's begin playing with potential design ideas.

Strong lines make a very noticeable contribution to the visual impact of a quilt. Lines have the power to direct attention toward or away from its various parts. They can affect the mood of the work by adding movement and excitement or contribute a quieter, mellower feel. For example, horizontal lines commonly create the impression of calm, tranquility and space. Strong vertical lines can give the feeling of importance, drama and height. Diagonals tend to indicate action or forward movement and tightly angled lines that constantly meet and cross each other give a dynamic, lively effect to the work.

Design A. This plaid style quilting design does nothing for the smaller boxes. Neither do the lines shown in the larger square shapes. The lines seem regimented and predictable while the top is more about color and whimsy, so they don't tell the same story – in other words, they aren't integrated.

Design B. This overall design idea fails to help unify the quilt. It looks choppy and out of context.

Design C. The diagonal lines in the larger flower boxes have great energy and the triple line of quilting subtly supports the importance of these larger squares. Single lines in the smaller squares resonate with the same energy and help to unify the flower-colored parts of the top. One would expect the overall look of a lawn to be less random than flowers, so straight lines in the green spaces works perfectly.

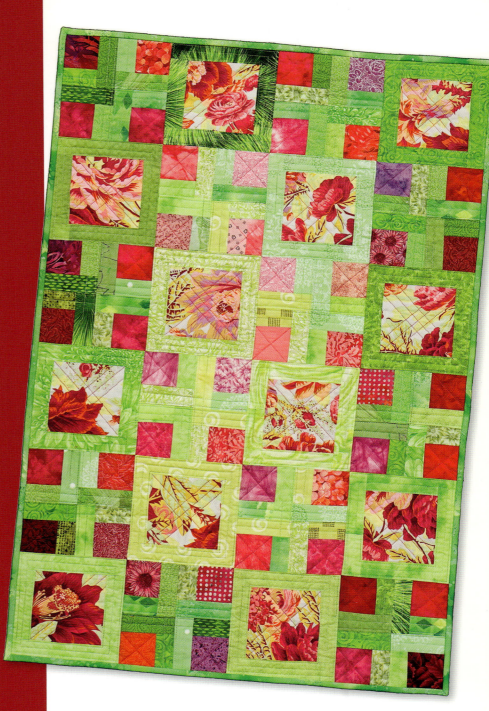

Sunday Brunch. The garden quilting idea works very well here. Design C is just right!

The same kind of line, running in different directions, can add interest to the overall quilting pattern. Repeated lines of parallel stitching on traditional quilts often changed direction upon reaching the outside border, thus highlighting the center or the border – or both!

Not All Lines Are Equally Visible

Variegated thread adds a come-and-go effect to a line of stitching. Where the value of the thread matches the value of the patch over which it is sewn, the thread will almost disappear. Where the thread contrasts with the patch it will be easily seen. A quilting design stitched with variegated thread will alternate between creating texture and creating a visible linear design.

"Now you see it, now you don't" stitching is an exciting design possibility. When thread crosses over fabrics of different colors and/or values, the line may blend with some sections and not with others. For example, if red thread travels across a white patch then across a red patch, the line can easily be seen against the white fabric but is barely noticeable against the red.

Another way of creating the "sometimes" option is to use variegated thread. This thread is available in values ranging from light to dark or color to color on the same spool. Stitched onto a quilt, the effect is for some parts of the line to disappear against the fabric and other parts to stand out. This lively come-and-go visibility engages our attention.

If a consistent thread presence is the goal, there are several techniques that make it easy. Changing thread color to match each patch crossed is one way to accomplish it. Machine quilters can use invisible thread – smoke colored for quilts with predominantly dark fabrics, clear for light-colored ones. Either machine or hand quilters might choose gray or beige thread that mostly blends with all of the different fabrics in the quilt top. Stitching a sample will tell you which thread color will achieve the visibility of line preferred on a particular quilt.

Tip!

I love the look of 'come and go' stitching. Just to make it interesting both to look at and for me to sew, I stitched yellow on yellow, pink on pink, and when I was feeling particularly whimsical, a yellow to pink variegated thread over both. Because of the subtle color choices, the thread adds lots of great texture without making a strong design statement.

Decoding the Magic of Lines

There are three basic qualities of any stitched line; visibility, style and scale. Understanding them lets us easily expand the range of potential designs we can create. Varying each of them opens an endless range of quilting ideas.

Visibility

The visibility of a line sewn by hand and a line stitched by machine are very different from one another. Knowing in advance how much a line will (or won't) be seen and how much texture the stitching will add to the surface takes much of the guess work out of the design process.

A subtle line is the unique quality of hand stitching. The hand quilter creates a series of thread dots on the surface of a quilt by carefully rocking the needle in and out of the quilt layers. The look of this line is a series of inconspicuous, bumpy indentations. Even with contrast between the darkness of the thread and the darkness of the patch over which the stitches run, the thread itself rarely dominates. At only a few feet from the quilt surface, we read texture, not line and color.

All about the subtleties of light, there isn't one specific section of this quilt top that demands to be highlighted by the quilting – a perfect opportunity to utilize an all-over design.

A bold, emphatic line is the inherent nature of machine quilting. Machine stitching puts a solid line of thread on the quilt top interrupted only by the merest dimpling where the bobbin thread loops up to form the stitch. Much more thread is visible with machine quilting than with hand quilting. Even when invisible thread is used, the line is crisper than the soft dots and dashes of hand quilting. Unless the machine quilter chooses to soften the effect by controlling the color, value (darkness) and weight of the thread, the look of machine stitching is the line itself.

Hand quilting and machine quilting produce very different but equally rewarding types of lines. Both can add depth and dimension to a quilt and create a richer visual experience for the viewer.

Topsy Turvey. *Straight line stitching adds lots of texture and it was quick and easy to sew. Marking was done with ¾" masking tape and a medium value, medium weight green thread allowed the play on light to shine through.*

Style

A straight line is the most basic quilting style. Pioneer quilters created a wide variety of easily stitched straight-line patterns for their quilts. Parallel lines and grids with their many variations, because of their timeless beauty and ease of stitching, are commonly used to this day. For a slightly more modern look, try varying the spacing, the orientation, or both. You might use noticeably uneven spacing, stitch straight lines that are much greater or less than a 45 degree angle to the seam line or stitch straight lines that are not parallel to each other.

Lines can be angular—jagged, zigzag, boxy, triangular or spiky. The angles can be varied to be either wide or narrow and repeated either regularly or randomly.

Another factor to consider in line style is length. Long lines and short lines have different design effects. Short lines can be very lively and unexpected. Long lines lend stability to a design and are often easier to stitch.

Overall designs in traditional hand quilting and most background filler designs are the same line repeated many times to form a pattern. The multitude of designs utilized by pioneer hand quilters are prime examples of repeated line designs: diagonal parallel lines, double parallel lines, fan, diagonal grids, on-grain grids, hanging diamonds, chevrons, etc.

The repeated character of these lines, requiring numerous starts and stops, is much easier for hand quilters than it is for machine quilters. The machine quilter will want to be sure the quilting has been designed so that starts and stops are reduced to the smallest possible number.

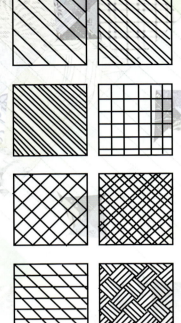

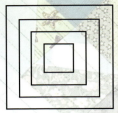
Hand quilting stitch

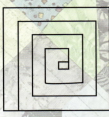
Machine quilter's version

While hand quilters can easily move between squares by slipping their needle between the layers and coming up to start on a new one, a machine quilter might want to modify the stitching design to eliminate as many starts and stops as possible.

Scale

Lines of quilting have scale. Scale refers to the distance between the lines. Lines can be placed very closely together or they can be widely spaced. Close spacing can look tidy as well as tight; wide spacing can appear either airy or hurried. In order to get the effect you desire, it's important to keep space between the stitched lines complimentary to your quilt top. The same spacing will not be right for every quilt. In fact, the same spacing may not be right for all areas of the same quilt.

Try out several spacings for your lines before settling on one or a combination of lines that is most flattering to your top. If you play around, your eye will tell you when you have come up with the most pleasing set of lines for the quilting design.

Tip!

The goal of providing adequate stitching doesn't mean that all squares have to be quilted identically. Here, the scale is appropriate in that the stitch lines are close enough together to fill the space even though each one is different.

Getting Started

Any stitching will change the appearance of the quilt top. The artistic goal of your quilting design is to control the texture and color while introducing lines and shapes that work with the pieced or appliquéd design.

How can you know if a design you are considering will be effective? One way is to make samples. If you are stitching by machine, samples are easily accomplished. If they increase the likelihood of choosing a design that works, they are worth the time and effort. You can also make sampling do double duty by testing batt and thread at the same time. If you are hand quilting, samples are possible but time consuming.

A great way to test a design before stitching is to draw it onto a piece of clear Duralar™ or Plexiglas™, either of which can be found in art supply stores or online. A piece about 18" by 24" is a good, workable size. Mark the edges of the semi-rigid plastic with a strip of tape so it can be easily seen. The tape indicates where the edges are so you know exactly where to stop drawing in order to avoid marking on your quilt top. Place it over your quilt, trace or freehand test patterns

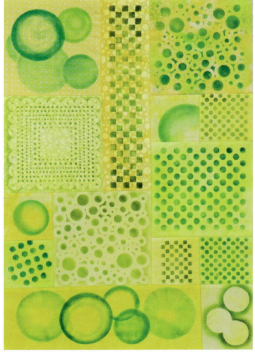

Two different strategies leap to mind for quilting this top. One is to acknowledge the different sections by quilting them individually; the other would be to give it an overall quilting design in order to unify the whole.

Design A. Well, question asked and answered! The drawing looks very busy and not in a good way. Not only does it fail to enhance the quilt, this design makes it look choppy and unsettling.

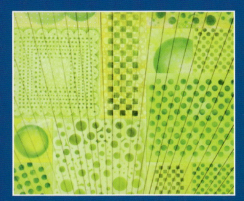

Design B. Radiating designs can be tricky to pull off because you need to be careful to make sure the quilting is fairly even over the entire surface. This design is a huge improvement over the first attempt but something isn't quite right. Vertical lines tend to convey an impression of power to the viewer. This many strong verticals give the overall feeling of aggression.

Design C. Love this idea! It solves the challenge of even quilting that radiating designs can present and the diagonal lines give an impression of cheerful liveliness while unifying the entire top into one dynamic whole.

Summertime. Knowing in advance that the quilting lines were going to be close together presented the opportunity to choose a batt with more loft that usual. The result is great texture. The design was marked with masking tape and quilted with a very fine thread.

directly onto the plastic with a Vis-à-Vis Wet Erase™ pen and take a look. This allows you to evaluate how the lines and shapes of your planned quilting design will relate to the pattern of your quilt top. You can erase and redraw lines repeatedly as this is a very durable material. Throughout this book, you will see photos of test patterns drawn on Duralar™ as a final quilt design takes shape.

By definition, quilting transforms a top into a quilt. So how do you know where to start in order to get the finished quilt you desire? Ask yourself what part of the quilt needs to be highlighted.

Straight lines that converge on a section will naturally draw the eye toward their center so you can utilize quilting to draw attention to a particular place.

Keep the space between your quilting lines complementary to your quilt block pattern while also considering the ultimate use of the finished product. If the background lines around a small pattern are too far apart, the pattern will seem lost. If the lines are quilted extremely close together on a large bed-sized quilt, the quilt can become a bit too stiff for comfortable use.

Stitching through the layers is a time-consuming process. Keep in mind that quilting shows better on light fabrics with little or no pattern than on most medium, dark, multi-colored and heavily patterned fabrics. Although machine quilting takes less time than hand quilting, a significant amount of effort is involved in both processes. For this reason, a general rule to keep in mind is: If quilting a particular area won't have a lot of artistic impact, consider keeping your stitching in those spots simple.

Think about the parts of your quilt. They may be quilted separately or all together or in any combination. Open yourself up to the possibility of new quilting schemes.

Borders offer more design possibilities. The fabrics may be quilted separately or together with the rest of the top. The designs should mirror any other lines used.

Santa is Coming to Town. *Changing the size, style or orientation of grid lines emphases the center motif. Here, two different kinds of straight lines, evenly distributed, allow the piece to hang straight and square and set off Santa, the most important part of the design.*

It's human nature for us to want to put more work into our favorite parts of a quilt which may lead us to quilt those areas more heavily than others. Ironically, heavily stitched areas generally appear to recede slightly while less quilted sections often 'pop' forward. So, if you quilt a row of blocks heavily and ignore the sashing in between, the sashing is the part the viewer is likely to notice first.

Adjacent borders can be treated singly or as a unit. For very narrow borders (1½ inches or less) quilting in the ditch (along the seams) can make the fabric ripple. A better choice is to stitch a simple line or two down the middle or slightly off to one side of these sections for a different effect.

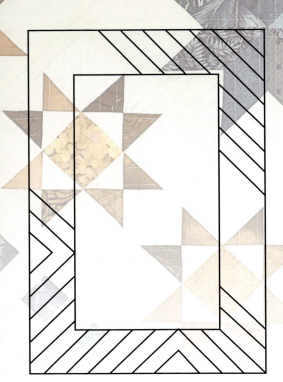

Diagonal lines quilted onto a border will look tidy only if you make sure each line is an exact continuation from one side of the quilt top to the other. The lines on the upper right section of this drawing can be problematic. Even exact line placement – which can be tricky – won't guarantee that it will look as you intend because sometimes the eye can be distracted by individual quilt blocks or fabric patterns and fooled into perceiving a line to be crooked or misplaced when it is not. The lines on the bottom left each take on a separate identity and don't completely depend on the line on the other side of the quilt top in order to look deliberately placed. A much easier way to succeed!

Lines parallel to the quilt edge can be tricky. If the lines stray even a tiny bit away from being perfectly parallel to both the binding and the center of the quilt (and they almost always do!) the viewer will likely see the whole thing as messy. In addition, this stitching tends to cause excessive rippling. To avoid these potential pitfalls, try running your stitched lines off the edge of the quilt. Not only is it likely to look better; as an added bonus your quilt edge will stay flatter.

The stars are the show! Straight line quilting will support the desired bold, graphic overall statement – even if filling this much white space with just the right quilting design seems a bit daunting at the initial planning stage.

Line Choices

None of the designs discussed here need to be stitched over the entire surface of your quilt. Utilize any line by itself or in combination with others on any part of the quilt top. This applies to borders, too, where the quilting may mirror the quilt blocks in the main part or take on a creative life of its own. If it appeals to you and satisfies the design needs of your quilt, by all means mix as many quilting line styles as you like.

Check for balance by turning the quilt over and looking carefully at the quilt backing. Without all of the quilt block distractions it's much easier to see the complete effect of the quilting design. It also becomes apparent if there are any areas you have missed or under-quilted.

Outline Quilting

Easily accomplished by a hand quilter, outline quilting is simply stitching around each patch of fabric. Stitching ¼" from the seam line assures that the quilter does not have to deal with the extra bulk of the seam allowance. With larger patches of fabric, double or triple lines might be necessary to both provide enough stitching and to keep the patch looking balanced. Machine quilters can certainly utilize this style to great effect – just be aware you are committing yourself to a multitude of starts and stops!

The size of a design needs to directly relate to the area it covers. This is particularly important when you are quilting in open areas such as plain quilt blocks, side and corner triangles, sashes and borders. The quilting design should look like it belongs, neither too big nor too small for the space.

Design A. *An angular stitch design emphasizes the center stars. The border idea is so different from the angles it distracts from rather than supports the stars. Another point against it is that this type of border design can be problematic. If each and every line doesn't match up precisely with the stitched lines on the opposite border, the overall effect will be messy. There's no point in creating future problems unnecessarily.*

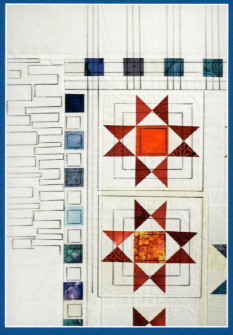

Design B. *Cutting off the points of the stars looks terrible. The design inside the little blue border squares looks great but the multitude of starts and stops required to machine stitch all those squares individually has little appeal. In the spirit of experimentation there are two different ideas sketched for the border. The plain straight lines don't provide enough quilting and have too little impact. The in-and-out cityscape looking border idea is a good one but doesn't quite work for this quilt because the only practical way to sew it is freehand and this very precisely pieced quilt needs something a little more formal to set it off. I'll use the cityscape quilting design another time.*

Design C. *Angular lines work for the blue stars but don't provide enough quilting for the red ones. The border idea is a winner. It is bold, graphic and literally points the eye toward the all-important center of the quilt top. The border could have been designed with nothing but the 1" angular, parallel lines but it would be tedious to mark and sew. Mixing in a few straight lines that run parallel to the quilt edge made it more fun to sew and ultimately more interesting for the viewer. Lines stitched parallel to a border can be challenging to keep looking straight and tidy. Notice these lines are short which sidesteps that issue.*

Albuquerque. *It's perfectly acceptable to combine the best parts of many designs. The idea for the stars comes from Design A. It accents the stars and there is enough stitching. The border design comes from Design B. Most of the design is stitched off the edge which helps to keep the quilt nice and square. This is a mark-as-you-go design done with masking tape.*

Design A. The vertical lines are too bold for the design. In addition, they look distressingly like rain.

Design B. This quilt is all about the zig zag, so highlighting it should look great, but too much of a good thing gets boring. The lavender parts need something a bit different in order to make them important, too.

Design C. The yellow zig zag, already trying to dominate the quilt, becomes even stronger with this design making it just too much. However, the calming effect of the horizontal lines in the lavender parts is very appealing and fits well with the mountains at dusk notion.

Vertical and Horizontal Lines

Single, double and triple parallel lines from side to side or top to bottom can be stitched over the quilt top. These lines can be evenly spaced or not depending on your needs and your overall quilting design.

Quilting inspiration can come from any number of places. This top puts me in mind of the Appalachian Mountains at that magical moment just before the sun retires for the evening. The yellow 'sun rays' are important but so too are the purple 'mountains'.

Evensong. Combining the best of both worlds, the finished quilt boasts the highlighted yellow zig zags as shown in Design B along with the horizontal lines of Design C.

Diagonal Lines

Diagonal lines can be stitched in one or both directions. The use of multiple lines can add depth and dimension.

Pat's Girls. There are just enough diagonal lines to hold the layers together while still adding visual interest. Notice that the lines are stitched right across the figures. Quilting off the edge of the quilt keeps the whole piece square and flat.

Many times a straight line crosshatch design is the only one stitched on an entire quilt. Stitch lines first in one direction and then in the opposite direction to form the box or crosshatch. This is often done with a one inch grid but can be utilized with any grid size you choose.

Plaid or Broken Plaid Lines

Similar to cross hatching but with more lines is the plaid or broken plaid design. A simple plaid design consists of double diagonal lines. A broken plaid is made by doubling or even tripling every other line.

A bold and graphic quilt top can often benefit from an equally bold and graphic quilting design. Subtle quilting would disappear and an opportunity to increase the 'wow' factor would be lost.

Design A. Too many lines interrupt the flow of this piece. Another issue is that the diagonals create a bit of a European cathedral stained-glass-window effect which doesn't mesh well with the intended air of exoticness.

Design B. Vertical lines on the orange fabric do nothing to support this quilts graphic look and the diagonal lines stitched on the dark print won't show enough for the desired graphic look.

Sometimes the fabric on the back of the quilt can offer the perfect inspiration. Bold diagonals will work very well and, as an added bonus, it is super easy to mark and stitch diagonal lines by utilizing this plaid fabric pattern.

Staggered Lines

Unevenly spaced parallel lines can be very interesting and make an excellent choice when done in both directions. Corners are particularly appealing where the lines cross one another. If these converging lines are made of different colored threads, a particularly bold design emerges.

Random Lines

Random lines produce a clean, modern feel. There is no right or wrong direction to take. Just make sure the quilting is fairly evenly spaced and go at it with gusto!

Marrakesh. *Diagonals tend to convey the notion of energy and excitement which is just right for this striking quilt. Using the fabric pattern on the back, this was stitched entirely from the back, first with a very thick purple thread wound on the bobbin and then a thin orange machine embroidery thread going the other direction.*

Marking Lines

Straight quilting requires marking lines of one kind or another to use as stitching guides. These days there is a bewildering profusion of marking tools, pens and pencils on the market meant for this purpose. If you have a favorite method or tool that has worked for you in the past, by all means use it. I think simple is best so let's explore some easy ways to quilt straight lines using inexpensive and readily available tools and techniques. For straight line quilting, I use the edge of the walking foot attachment, the quilting guide that comes with it, painters tape, a chalk wheel or quilting paper.

Inexpensive and effective marking tools include painter's tape, quilting paper and a white chalk wheel.

Painters Tape

Painter's tape (often blue but it does come in other colors) can keep lines right where they are wanted and is available in a variety of convenient widths ranging from 1/4" up to 3". Lay different sizes next to each other to create whatever space you choose between your stitch lines.

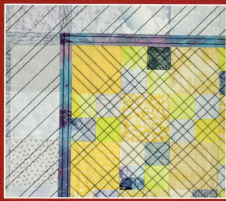

Design A. *This many lines may not be necessary. Also, the border quilting would need very exact placement to make sure the lines of stitching exactly match up across the quilt from one border all the way across to another or the result won't look quite right.*

Design B. *The straight lines in the center have potential, but the diagonal lines in the border will be tedious to mark accurately and they add another design element that won't show well enough to warrant the effort.*

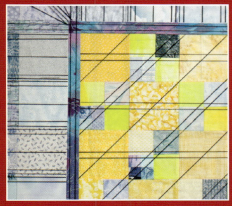

Design C. *This idea is somewhat the reverse of Design B as it moves the diagonal lines to the center and puts the verticals and horizontals on the edge. Combined in this way, the two design elements look a bit strident and not pleasing to the eye.*

Sun Break. *The straight line design shown in the quilt center in Design B was the winner and the border design was borrowed from the quilt, 'Albuquerque'. Notice the grid on the border is spaced closer together than the one in the center. More heavily quilted areas appear to recede slightly so this technique moves the center forward in importance. The center was marked with masking tape and stitched with yellow quilting thread. The border was marked with masking tape and free motion quilted with blue quilting thread.*

Start by laying the tape on the quilt top in approximately the correct place so you can see which basting pins are going to be in the way. Once those few pins have been removed, reapply the tape carefully so the positioning is precise. The low tack of the painter's tape will stick nicely but won't leave a residue on your quilt with just a minimum of care. It's generally a good idea to remove the tape at the end of each day. We may plan to return to stitching the first thing in the morning, but sometimes life gets in the way and a week or two flies by. If you have already removed the tape your quilt will be safely waiting for you without any possibility of residue.

The medium color values in this top means the quilting design won't show as much as it would on a lighter-colored one. A simple quilting design will add a beautiful texture and more dramatic stitching designs can be saved for another quilt top where that effort will show to better effect.

To sew a single-stitch straight line design, stitch along both sides of the taped 'stripe' you have already placed on the quilt top. If you accidentally stitch over the top of the tape, just use tweezers to pull away the small bits that will resist removal. When you complete one row, realign the tape with the line you have just finished stitching. Then quilt the next line.
Sewing a row of straight lines means the tape needs to be repositioned along the stitched line and a new line of stitching sewn, repeating the process across the quilt. You will have to replace the tape eventually when it isn't sticky enough to maintain an accurate line.

Quilting Paper

One easy way to mark a quilting pattern is to use Golden Threads Quilting Paper™. The paper is transparent enough to see through for exact design placement on the quilt. Tape it in place, stitch along your drawn lines and easily tear it away when you are done. There may be a very few insignificant remnants to clean up but it only takes a second or two to do. Use a permanent pen to trace the design onto the paper so there's no chance of the marks staining the needle as it passes through the paper and, in turn, marring the fabric.

To make a repeated pattern for a quilt, stack up to 15 sheets of paper with the traced pattern design on top. Pin the layers together to hold them securely in position and stitch with no thread in your sewing machine along the drawn line. You will create an identical perforated pattern on each sheet.
The bonus is that these perforated sheets are much easier to remove.

The playful boxes are an important part of the design and the quilting needs to emphasize them.

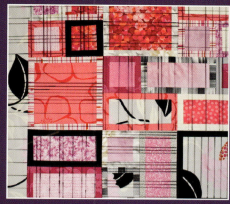

Design A. *All these lines obscure the boxes and visually 'flatten' them.*

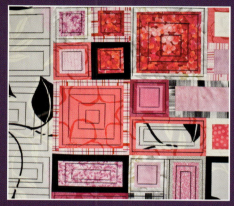

Design B. *Concentric boxes look great but would be problematic to stitch because of the many (and tedious!) starts and stops. If this was the only way to incorporate square-shaped quilting it would be worth considering but a bit of redesign can make this much easier to machine stitch.*

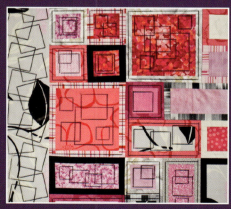

Design C. *A perfect compromise! The fabric squares are highlighted with multiple squares in the quilting design and because most of the boxes overlap there are far fewer starts, stops and knots to tie. This is a great example of altering a design to make it easier to machine quilt. One square is stitched then, where it overlaps a new one, the top is turned and a new square stitched. Notice that the border is a continuous line design, too.*

Fashion Forward. *The Design C quilting design is just right. As intended, the fabric squares are highlighted and the tumbling squares around the outside edge provide a perfect balance between the center squares and the flowing vines in the border fabric. This was marked using Golden Threads Quilting Paper™, which is a wonderful product to use in making your own tear-away stencils. It tears away cleanly and easily without pulling out any stitches.*

White Chalk Wheel

Chalk comes in colors other than white. Unfortunately, although lines drawn with darker colors may be more visible, the dyes with which the colors are made can sometimes be difficult to remove from your finished quilt.

The small serrated wheel inside the tip easily draws very fine chalk lines that will simply brush white chalk away. Marking one small section at a time will help the chalk stay in plain sight. Otherwise, as you handle the quilt, the chalk may be inadvertently brushed off and you will need to mark it again.

One important thing to keep in mind is that chalk will heat-set. Ironing over it makes it difficult if not impossible to remove.

No Marking

Not every quilting design has to be marked. Neither marking nor having to remove the marks after stitching shortens the time it takes to finish a quilt and can be a really fun exercise in creativity. When planning to do free-motion stitching, work the design out first with pencil and paper to be sure you like it. In fact, doing this is a great warm-up exercise. Free-motion stitching can be utilized for an overall design for the quilt top or it can be easily combined with other methods.

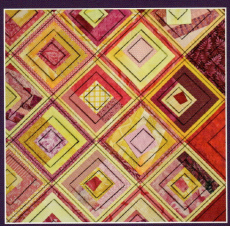

Design A. Quilts look best when evenly stitched over the entire surface, including the sashing. Starting with simple straight line in the sashing, squares of some kind seemed like a good possibility for the blocks.

Design B. Straight lines in the narrow sashing are a given, free motion squares and triangles fill up the empty spaces perfectly and look like they will be a lot of fun to sew – which is always a plus!

Uneven squares in different color values means the quilting won't show very much, making this top a perfect candidate for no marking, free-hand style quilting.

Design C. Too many lines going in too many directions makes for an awkward looking design.

Ladies Laughing. Quilted as shown in design B, the pink and yellow threads shine through. No marking was used here, just free style quilting.

In Conclusion...

Your quilt top is beautiful – and the quilting is the delicious frosting on the cake! Look over the suggestions and ideas presented here and then let the feel of your quilt and your unique artistic interpretation play out in your work. The result? Pure genius!